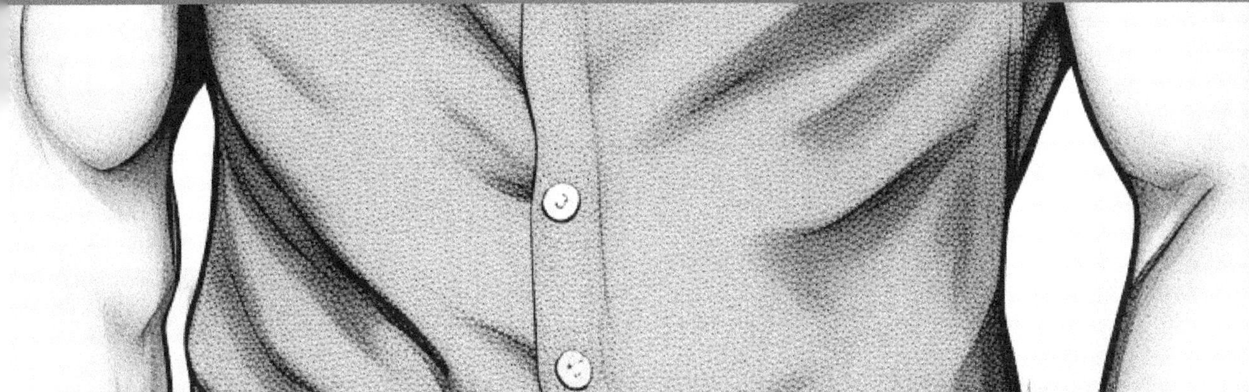
and this fuck boy
belongs to:

the one
that
eats all
your food

you don't mind right babe?
THE ONE THAT SCROLLS THROUGH PORN ON YOUR COMPUTER

the one that
looks like
Aquaman

the glorified
bike
messenger

the
one
that's
just a
perv

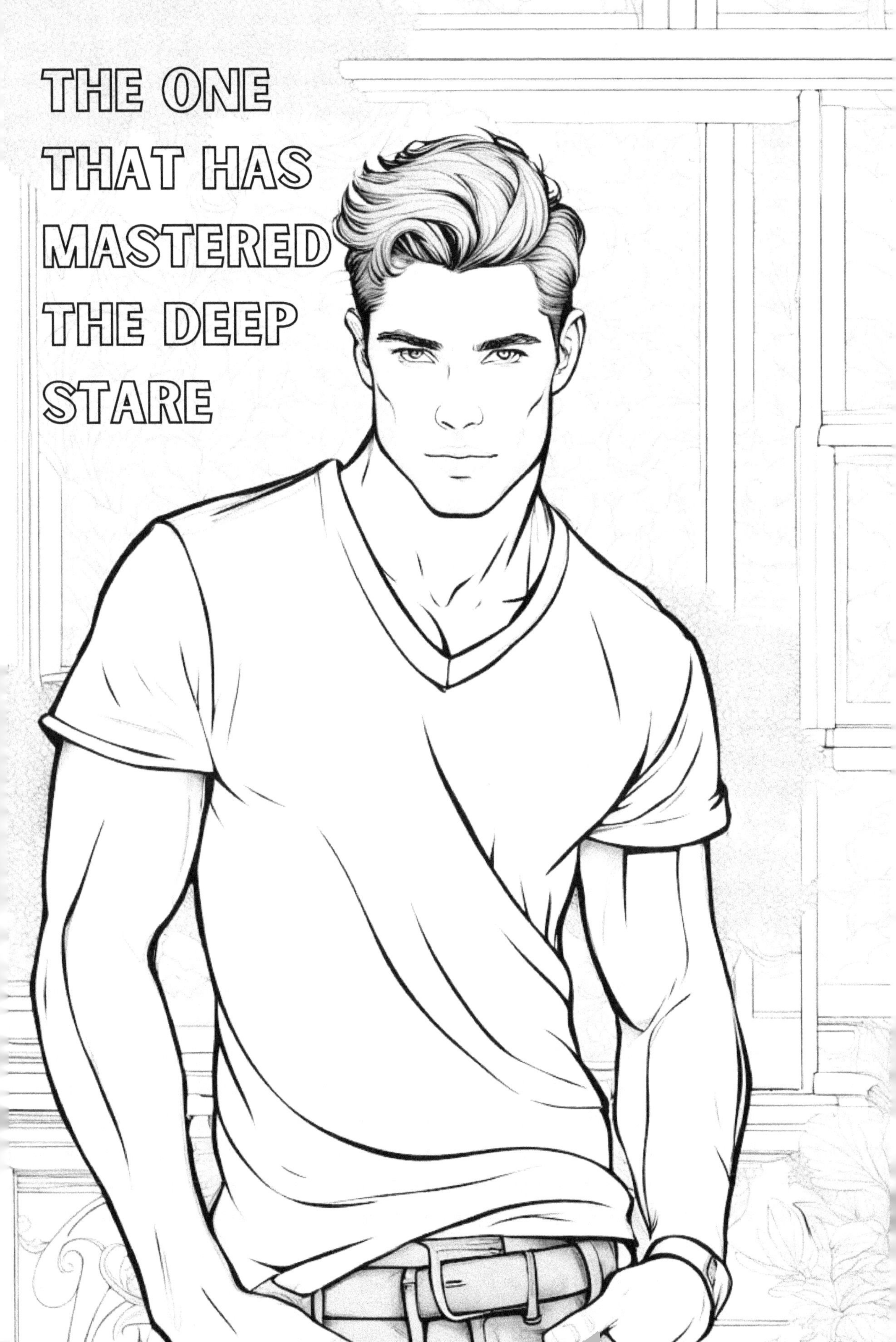
THE ONE
THAT HAS
MASTERED
THE DEEP
STARE

THE ONE
THAT
LOVES
THE CHASE

the one that pretends he's a deep thinker

are your
friends
coming?

the one
that
flexes at
all times

the one that eats cereal for dinner

the one
that's
heading
to the
gym

THE ONE
WITH
WORK IN
THE
MORNING

THE JOCK

THE ONE IN
COLLEGE
BUT REALLY
JUST TO
BANG CHICKS

the one
that thinks
all women
want him

the one
you
thought
you could
change

the
one
with
abs for
days

the one
that can
dance

the one
that
smokes

Bathroom
Selfie

the one
with
money

3:18 AM
WYD
?

OH, you
have a
podcast?

the one with a hookah

Mr. Gray

the one
that
thinks
he's
Drake

Why do you look
like a superhero?

the one in a band

the other one in a band

Its just
my sister

the
bro

THE ONE
THAT
FORGETS
HIS
WALLET

the young one

THE
ONE
THAT
TALKS
ABOUT
HIS EX

BUT HE
LOOKS
AT YOU
LIKE THAT